Community Helpers

Dentists

by Dee Ready

Content Consultant:
Isabel Garcia, D.D.S., M.P.H.
National Institute of Dental Research

Bridgestone Books
an imprint of Capstone Press

Bridgestone Books are published by Capstone Press
151 Good Counsel Drive, P.O. Box 669, Mankato, Minnesota 56002
http://www.capstone-press.com

Library of Congress Cataloging-in-Publication Data
Ready, Dee.
  Dentists/by Dee Ready.
  p. cm.—(Community helpers)
  Includes bibliographical references and index.
  Summary: Explains the clothing, tools, schooling, and work of dentists.
  ISBN 1-56065-558-5
  1.Dentists—Juvenile literature. 2. Dentistry—Juvenile literature.
[1. Dentists. 2. Dental Care. 3. Occupations.] I. Title. II. Series: Community
helpers (Mankato, Minn.)
RK63.R43   1998
617.6—dc21
                           97-6006
                               CIP
                               AC

Table of Contents

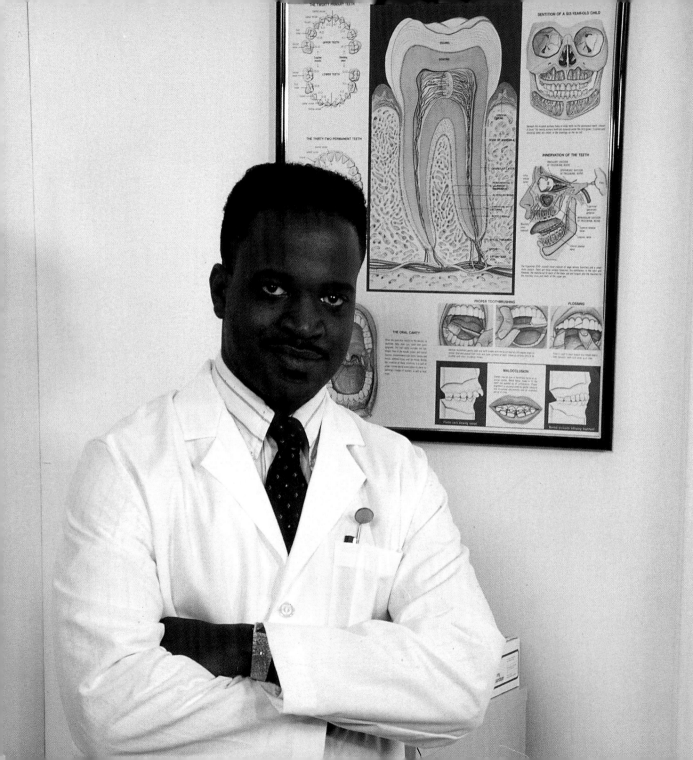

Dentists

Dentists help people with their teeth. Dentists fix teeth. They help keep people's teeth healthy, too. People go to dentists for examinations. An examination is a checkup to see if teeth are healthy.

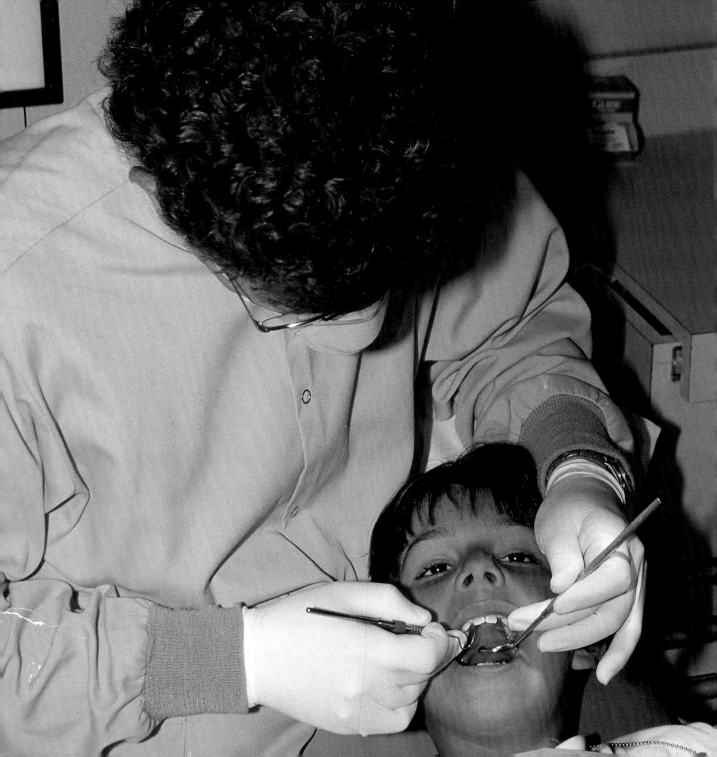

What Dentists Do

Dentists look for cavities. A cavity is a hole in a tooth. Dentists fix cavities they find. They also check to see if gums are healthy. Gums are the soft skin around teeth.

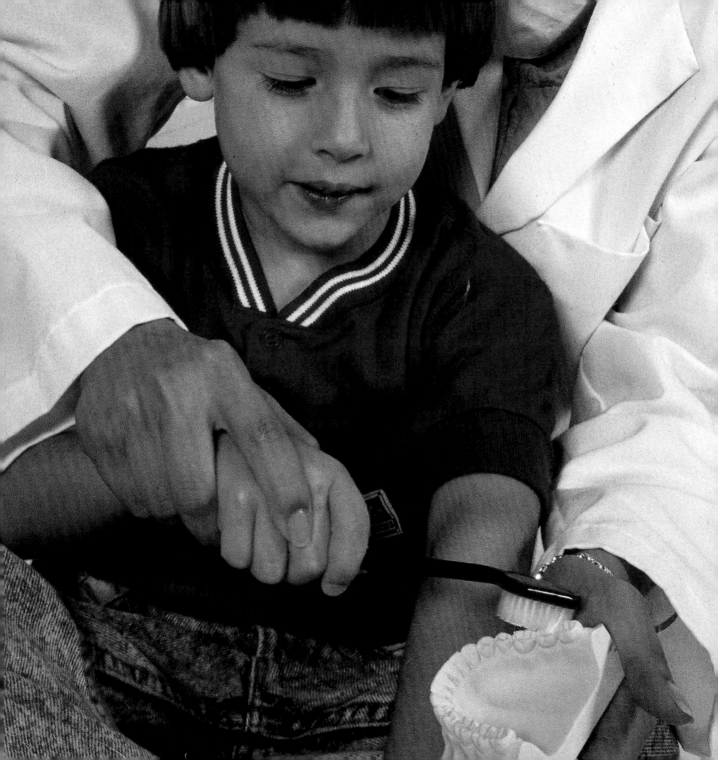

Different Kinds of Dentists

Many dentists fix cavities. Some dentists fix teeth that are crooked. Other dentists fix only children's teeth. They are called pediatric dentists. These dentists show children how to care for their teeth.

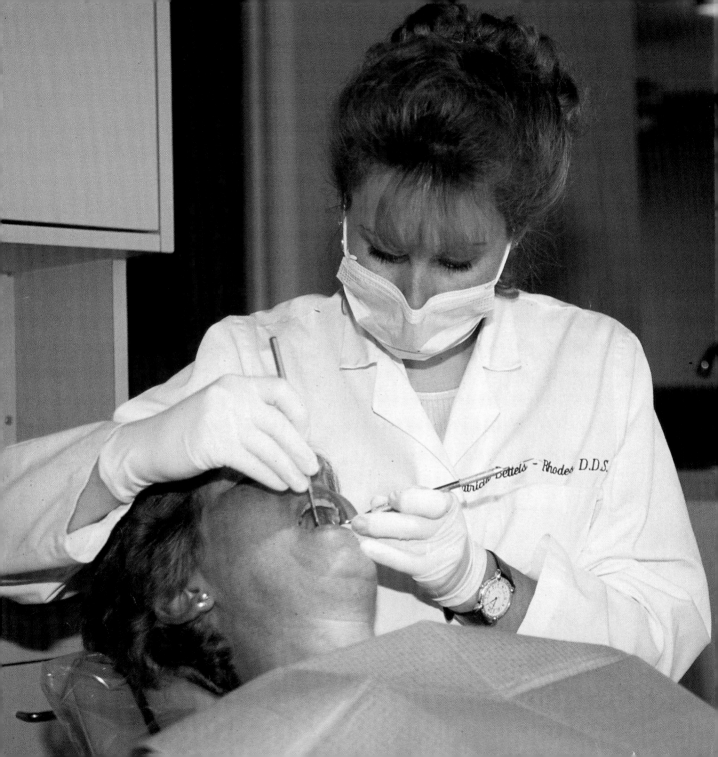

What Dentists Wear

Many dentists wear special gloves. They wear masks over their mouths, too. The masks and gloves help everyone stay healthy. Many dentists also wear white coats over their clothes.

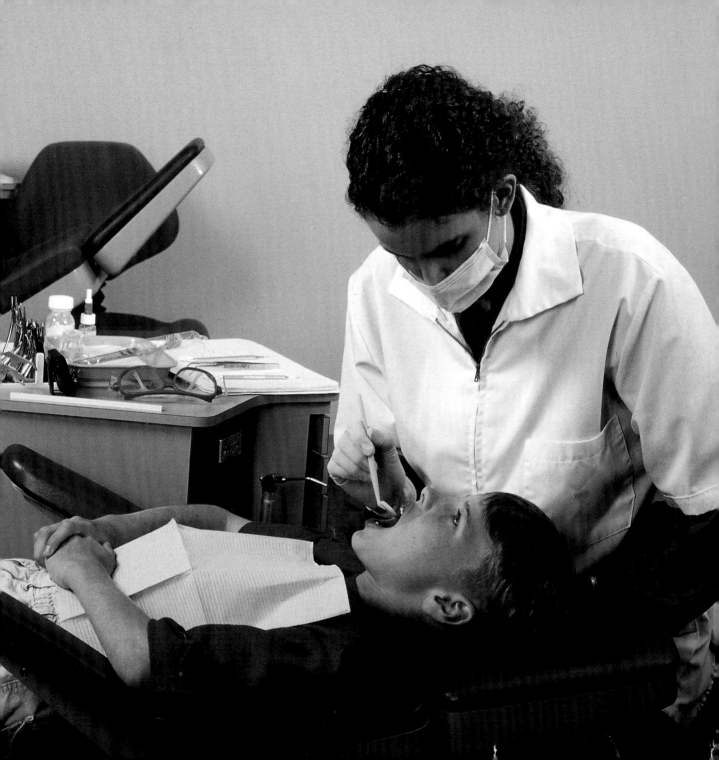

Tools Dentists Use

Dentists use small mirrors to look at teeth. They use special machines that take pictures of teeth. These pictures help dentists find cavities. Other dental tools help dentists fix cavities.

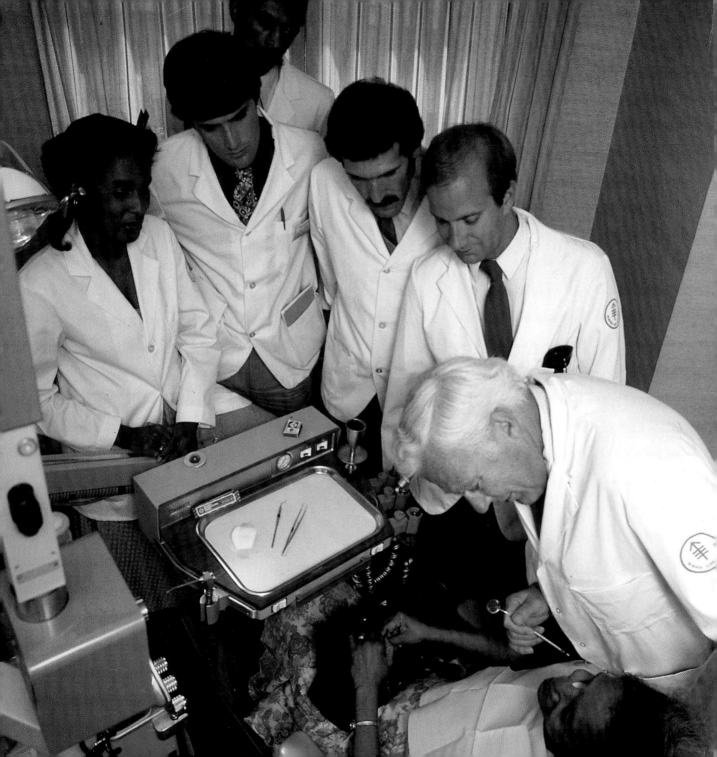

Dentists and School

All dentists go to college and dental school. They go to these schools for eight years or more. They learn how to keep teeth and gums healthy. They learn how to fix teeth, too.

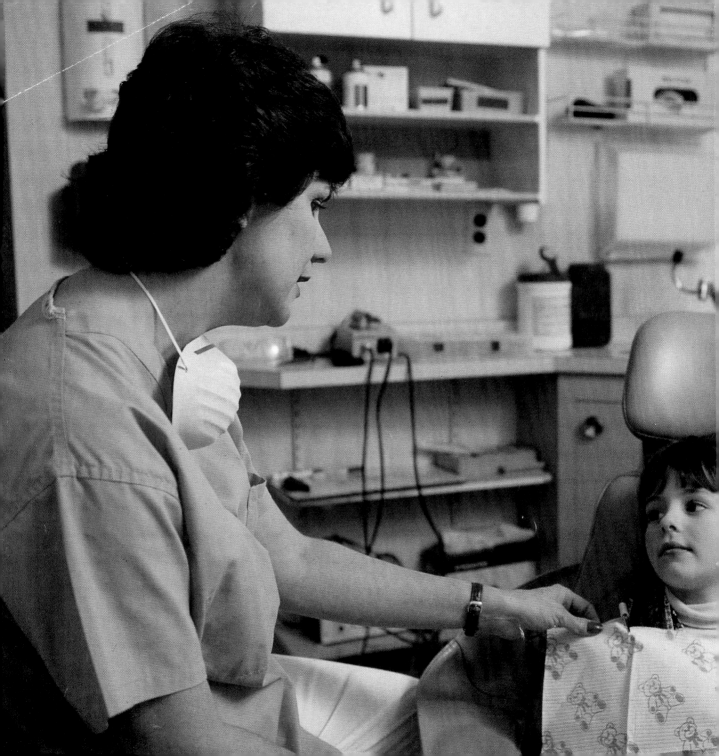

Where Dentists Work

Most dentists work in their own offices. Other dentists work in clinics. All dentists have examination rooms. These rooms have dental chairs and dental tools.

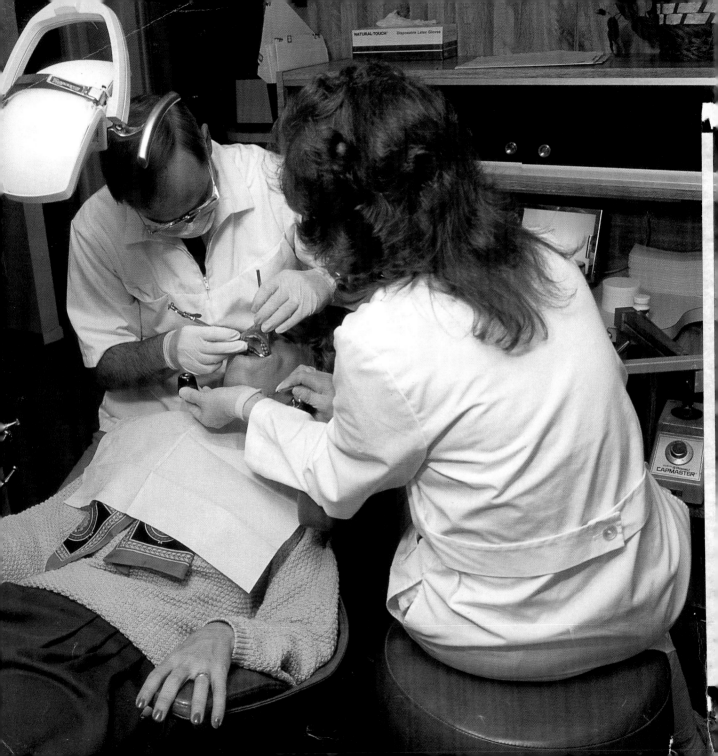

People Who Help Dentists

Dental assistants work directly with dentists. Other people called dental hygienists clean people's teeth. They also show people how to brush and floss. Floss means to clean between teeth with a special string.

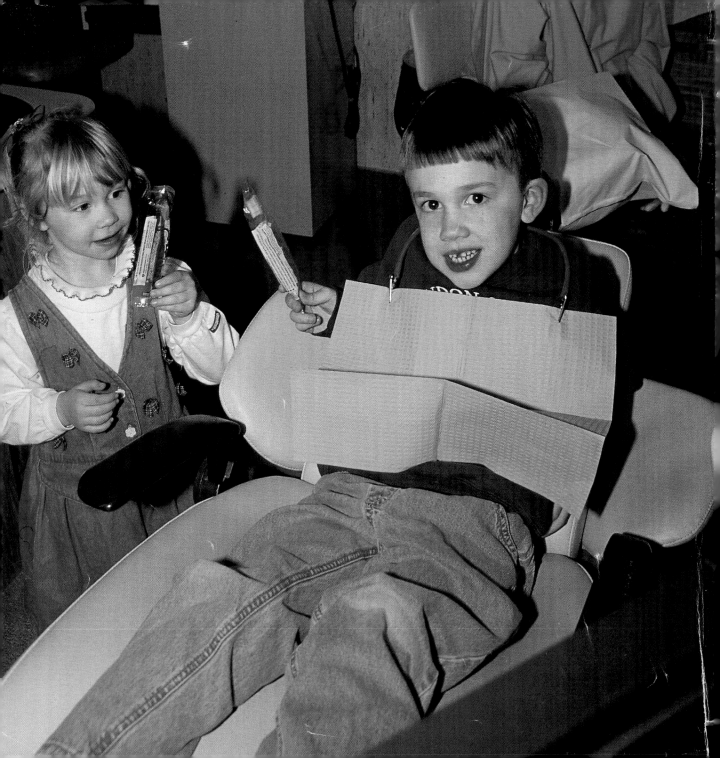

Dentists Help People

Dentists keep people's teeth healthy. They fix people's teeth. They tell people what foods are good for teeth. Strong and healthy teeth can last a lifetime.

Hands On: Count Teeth

The number of teeth you have changes as you grow. A baby has very few teeth. Adults have many teeth. Sometimes older adults do not have any real teeth. Dentists give them false teeth.

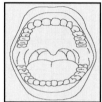

You can compare how many teeth people you know have. Be sure to wash your hands if you have to touch someone's teeth.

1. Count a baby's teeth. Write the number down on paper.
2. Count your own teeth. Use a mirror to see them all. Write the number down.
3. Count an adult's (20 to 49 years old) teeth. Write the number down.
4. Count an older adult's (50 years and older) teeth. Ask them how many of their teeth are real. Write down how many are real and not real.

Children between ages six and 13 have 20 to 24 teeth. Most adults have 24 to 32 teeth.

Words to Know

cavity (KAV-uh-tee)—a hole in a tooth
college (KOL-ij)—a school where students study after high school
examination (eg-zam-uh-NAY-shuhn)—a checkup to see if a person's teeth are healthy
floss (FLAWSS)—to clean between the teeth with thin string called dental floss
gums (GUHMS)—the soft skin around teeth

Read More

Frost, Helen. *Going to the Dentist*. Dental Health. Mankato, Minn.: Pebble Books, 1999.

James, Robert. *Dentists: People Who Care for Our Teeth*. Vero Beach, Fla.: Rourke, 1995.

Internet Sites

The Wisdom Tooth
http://www.umanitoba.ca/outreach/wisdomtooth/
Wizard of the Magical Os
http://www.magicalos.com

Index